SCORPIONS

by Vicky Franchino

Children's Press®

An Imprint of Scholastic Inc.

New York   Toronto   London   Auckland   Sydney
Mexico City   New Delhi   Hong Kong
Danbury, Connecticut

Content Consultant
Dr. Stephen S. Ditchkoff
Professor of Wildlife Sciences
Auburn University
Auburn, Alabama

Photographs ©: Alamy Images: 18, 19 (Bruce Farnsworth), 38,
39 (shootnikonrawstock), 10, 11 (ZUMA Press, Inc); Dreamstime/
Redking: 2 background, 3 background, 44, 45; Getty Images: 26, 27
(De Agostini), 4, 5, 30, 31 (Paul Zahl/National Geographic/Getty
Images); Media Bakery/Anthony Bannister: 20, 21; Newscom/Anthony
Bannister/NHPA/Photoshot: 40, 41; Science Source: 22, 23 (Daniel
Heuclin), cover (Michel Gunther), 1, 14, 15, 46 (Michel Gunther), 12,
13 (Raul Gonzalez), 32, 33 (Sinclair Stammers); Superstock, Inc.: 36,
37 (Animals Animals), 6, 7 (Biosphoto), 8, 9 (Ephotocorp), 28, 29
(Minden Pictures), 2 main, 3 main, 24, 25 (Mint Images), 34, 35
(Tom Brakefield), 16, 17 (Wayne Lynch/All Canada Photos).

Map by Bob Italiano

Library of Congress Cataloging-in-Publication Data
Franchino, Vicky, author.
  Scorpions / by Vicky Franchino.
      pages cm. — (Nature's children)
  Summary: "This book details the life and habits of scorpions."—
Provided by publisher.
  Audience: Ages 9–12.
  Audience: Grades 4 to 6.
  Includes bibliographical references and index.
  ISBN 978-0-531-21169-4 (library binding) —
ISBN 978-0-531-21188-5 (pbk.)
1. Scorpions—Juvenile literature. I. Title. II. Series: Nature's children
(New York, N.Y.)
  QL458.7.F73 2015
  595.4'6—dc23   2014029887

All rights reserved. Published in 2015 by Children's Press, an imprint
of Scholastic Inc. 56596094 5/15

Printed in China 62
SCHOLASTIC, CHILDREN'S PRESS, and associated logos are
trademarks and/or registered trademarks of Scholastic Inc.

1 2 3 4 5 6 7 8 9 10 R 24 23 22 21 20 19 18 17 16 15

Scorpions

Class	Arachnida
Order	Scorpiones
Family	17 families
Genera	More than 150
Species	More than 1,500
World distribution	Found on every continent except Antarctica
Habitats	Deserts, forests, rain forests, grasslands, seashores, mountains
Distinctive physical characteristics	Two claws for holding prey and tearing food; four pairs of legs; curved, segmented tail with a stinger at the end; average body length of around 6 inches (15.2 centimeters)
Habits	Nocturnal and sensitive to light; usually solitary except when mating; typically waits for food to pass by instead of actively hunting
Diet	Carnivorous; eats insects and arachnids (including other scorpions); some larger species also eat rodents, birds, lizards, and snakes

SCORPIONS

Contents

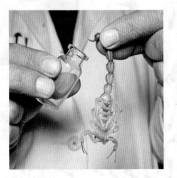

CHAPTER 1

Waiting for Dinner

The desert night is dark and still. Moonlight shines over the barren landscape. A gentle wind blows as clouds glide across the sky. A beetle dashes out from under a rock in search of a midnight meal. The beetle is not the only hungry creature in the desert tonight. Before it knows what's happened, a claw reaches out of the darkness and closes around the beetle's body. It's a scorpion! This ferocious **predator** has waited patiently for its dinner to appear.

As the beetle struggles to break free, the scorpion's tail curves over its head. At the tip of the tail is a poisonous stinger. It stabs the beetle over and over. **Venom** floods into the beetle's body. As the beetle dies, the hungry scorpion begins to feast.

A yellow scorpion stings an insect with its venomous tail.

8

Not an Insect

Scorpions might seem like insects, but they are actually a type of animal called an arachnid. There are a few simple ways to tell them apart. All insects have six legs, but arachnids have eight. An insect has three body segments, but an arachnid has only two. Many insects have wings and antennae. Arachnids have neither.

One thing that insects and arachnids have in common is that they don't have skeletons. Instead, they have a hard outer covering called an **exoskeleton**. The exoskeleton supports and protects an arachnid's body.

Scorpions can be found all over the world. They live in deserts, grasslands, forests, and caves, and along seashores. They have even been discovered under rocks high up in the snowy Himalayan and Andes mountains. Antarctica is the only continent without scorpions.

FUN FACT! Scientists have discovered frozen scorpions that were still alive once they thawed out!

The Asian forest scorpion lives in the rain forests of southeast Asia.

Many Kinds of Scorpions

Scientists have discovered more than 1,500 scorpion **species**. One of the largest is the emperor scorpion. This huge scorpion is found in West Africa. It can grow up to 8 inches (20 centimeters) long. That's about the width of a dinner plate! Although they might look scary, emperor scorpions are really quite mild-mannered. Some people even keep them as pets.

The smallest scorpions are only 0.5 inches (1.3 cm) long. They can fit on a person's fingernail. But don't be fooled by a scorpion's size! Many small scorpions are very dangerous. All scorpions have poisonous venom. Even small ones can often **paralyze** or kill a much larger animal.

Adult male
6 ft. (1.8 m)

Smallest scorpion
0.5 in. (1.3 cm) long

Largest scorpion
8 in. (20 cm) long

Even though emperor scorpions do not usually sting people, they should still be handled with care.

CHAPTER 2

The Scorpion's Body

A scorpion's body is divided into two main sections. The front section is called the cephalothorax. The scorpion's head, claws, and jaws are all part of the cephalothorax. A protective shell called a carapace covers the top of the cephalothorax.

The scorpion's eyes are located on its head. Most scorpions have one main set of eyes in the middle, plus two to five sets of smaller eyes called ocelli on the sides.

Each of a scorpion's two pedipalps, or claws, ends in a strong pincer. The pedipalps have several important jobs. The scorpion uses them to protect itself and find its way around. It also uses them to catch and hold on to prey.

Near the scorpion's mouth are strong fangs called chelicerae. They help the scorpion grab and crush its prey. The scorpion also uses these fangs to tear off pieces of food while it is eating.

A scorpion can have up to 12 eyes.

The Back End

The back section of a scorpion's body is called the **abdomen**. This is where most of a scorpion's internal **organs** are located.

On the underside of the abdomen are small holes called spiracles. They are attached to the four sets of book lungs inside the scorpion's body. Book lungs are made of layers that look like book pages. Air comes into the scorpion's body through the spiracles. The book lungs absorb oxygen from the air and remove carbon dioxide from the scorpion's body. Carbon dioxide leaves the body through the spiracles.

The abdomen is also where the scorpion's legs are found. Scorpions have four pairs of legs. Each leg ends in a set of tiny claws. These claws help the scorpion grip the ground as it moves.

FUN FACT! Scorpions usually live between three and eight years. Some species survive for twenty-five years or more.

A scorpion's abdomen is much larger than its cephalothorax.

16

A Terrifying Tail

The tail at the end of a scorpion's abdomen is very narrow and has six sections. The last section is the one that gets the most attention. It's where the scorpion's poisonous stinger is located!

The scorpion uses its stinger to attack prey and protect itself from predators. The stinger is found at the tip of the telson. The telson is shaped like a bulb. It holds two sacs full of venom. Small tubes carry this venom to the scorpion's stinger. The venom contains poisons that affect the nervous system. The scorpion uses its venom to paralyze or kill its victims.

Some scientists think there's a link between the strength of a scorpion's venom and the size and power of its pedipalps. They believe that a small scorpion with weak pincers will have stronger venom and a scorpion with powerful pincers will have weaker venom. Other scientists disagree. To be safe, it's always best to assume that any scorpion can mean trouble!

A droplet of venom hangs from the tip of a scorpion's stinger.

A Special Kind of Protection

A scorpion's exoskeleton is like a suit of armor. It's made of many small, hard sections. A flexible material connects the hard sections. This design protects the scorpion but still allows it to move.

Scientists have discovered a very interesting thing about the exoskeleton: it glows in the dark! Chemicals in the scorpion's exoskeleton cause it to glow under natural light. No one is entirely sure why this happens.

One theory is that the glow tells scorpions when it's too bright to be outside. Scorpions do not like to be in strong light. A glowing body is a warning that the light is too bright and they should hide. Scientists have found that scorpions move more slowly under bright lights. This makes them easy prey for predators. Another theory is that the glow helps scorpions find one another.

FUN FACT! A scorpion's glow is helpful to people, too. With a special flashlight, people can easily find scorpions and study their habits.

Scientists are still trying to discover exactly why scorpions glow.

Spectacular Senses

Even though scorpions can have as many as 12 eyes, their vision actually isn't very good. So how do scorpions find food and avoid becoming a predator's next meal? They have special features that allow them to rely on their sense of touch.

On the tips of the scorpion's legs are small organs that feel vibrations in the ground. These vibrations let a scorpion know if another animal is walking nearby. Sometimes this animal might be the scorpion's next meal. Other times it might be a dangerous predator looking to snack on the scorpion!

A scattering of hairs called setae grow from a scorpion's legs and pedipalps. Setae can feel vibrations in the air. This tells the scorpion what direction another creature is coming from. If a scorpion lives in a sandy place, setae also have another job to do. They help keep the scorpion from sinking into the sand.

A scorpion's pedipalps are covered in special hairs that feel vibrations.

Dinnertime

Scorpions are **carnivores**. That means they eat animals. A scorpion's preferred prey varies from species to species. Insects and arachnids are typically on a scorpion's dinner menu. One of their favorite foods is other scorpions! Larger scorpions might also eat lizards, mice, and snakes.

Most scorpions are nocturnal. They hide in burrows or under rocks or tree bark. This protects their sensitive eyes from sunlight and their bodies from drying out. When it's dark, they come out for dinner.

Some scorpions search for food, but most wait for food to come to them. Sometimes they'll wait for hours! A waiting scorpion sits absolutely still. When vibrations tell it an animal is near, the scorpion reaches out and grabs the animal with its pincers. Sometimes the scorpion attacks prey with its stinger, too.

A scorpion doesn't chew its food. Instead, it releases a substance that turns the inner parts of its prey into liquid. Then the scorpion sucks up its soupy meal.

A scorpion dines on a gecko in the Sahara Desert.

Able to Adapt

Scorpions can adapt to changes in the world around them. If the weather becomes too dry or cold, a scorpion might slow its metabolism and go into a dormant state. This allows the scorpion to live on less food and water and survive colder temperatures.

Some scorpions can also produce more than one type of venom. They make weak venom that can stun enemies and stronger venom that can paralyze or kill. Why is it important to have two choices? It takes a lot of energy and time for the scorpion's body to produce the stronger venom. The scorpion doesn't want to waste its strong venom if all it needs to do is frighten an enemy away. This variety lets scorpions handle many types of prey and predators in various situations.

FUN FACT! Some scorpions can go an entire year between meals.

Scorpions can survive in extremely dry climates.

CHAPTER 3

The Mating Dance

Scorpions do not usually spend much time together. The only time adult scorpions aren't alone is when they come together to mate. A female scorpion tells a male she's ready to mate by spreading chemicals called pheromones on the ground. A male scorpion uses organs on the bottom of its body to find these chemicals. These organs are called pectines. Pectines are shaped like a comb. As they brush against the ground, the male scorpion can follow the female's trail.

When a male scorpion finds a female, he grabs her pedipalps and twirls her around in a kind of dance. As they dance, the male uses his pectines to find a smooth surface on the ground where he can deposit a sticky clump of material called spermatophore. The male scorpion dances the female over this clump, and it enters her body through an opening on her underside.

A scorpion mating dance can sometimes last for hours.

Waiting for Babies

Some of the spermatophore mixes with the female's eggs, and babies start to form. The rest goes into a special sac in the female and is stored for later use. As a result, the female scorpion can produce four or five **litters** after mating just one time.

How long does it take a scorpion baby to be born? It depends on the species. Some scorpions develop in a few months. Others can take as long as one and a half years to be born.

Scorpions are viviparous. This means the babies develop inside the mother and are born alive instead of hatching from eggs. When it's time for the babies to be born, they leave the mother's body through the same opening where the spermatophore was absorbed. The mother uses her legs to catch the babies and protect them as they fall from her body. An average litter contains around 25 scorplings. However, as many as 100 scorpion babies can be born at once.

Male scorpions do not help females care for their young.

Make Way for Scorplings!

Newborn scorplings look like miniature versions of their parents. They are tiny, white, and helpless. They cannot produce venom, and their exoskeletons are very soft.

Scorplings climb up on their mother's back immediately after birth. During their first days of life, scorplings get their food from yolk material inside their bodies. They absorb water through their mother's exoskeleton. The mother scorpion carries her babies wherever she goes.

After about two weeks, a scorpling grows too big for its first exoskeleton. The exoskeleton cracks open and the scorpling crawls out with a new exoskeleton. The scorplings leave the safety of their mother's back and begin life on their own. This is a dangerous time for them. They are still small, and their exoskeleton needs to harden. They are easy targets for predators. Once a scorpion has grown and **molted** five to seven times, it is an adult.

Young scorpions are vulnerable to attacks from other animals as they are molting.

CHAPTER 4

A Prehistoric Giant

Scorpions' relatives have walked the earth—and maybe lived in the sea—for more than 400 million years. **Paleontologists** learn about ancient scorpions from **fossils.**

Sometimes, paleontologists find a fossil from only one part of an animal's body. They have to make educated guesses about what the rest of the animal looked like. In 2007, scientists discovered the fossil of a huge sea scorpion claw in Germany. Based on this claw, scientists estimated there was once a scorpion that was about 8.2 feet (2.5 meters) long. It is the largest **arthropod** scientists have ever found. Modern scorpions aren't very closely related to this ancient creature. However, scientists believe they had a shared **ancestor** at some point.

In Scotland, researchers found a fossil that showed the track of an ancient scorpion's tail and three rows of footprints. This scorpion was about 6.6 feet (2 m) long and 3.3 feet (1 m) wide. This fossil helped prove that sea scorpions spent at least some of their time on land.

This fossil of a sea-dwelling scorpion ancestor is around 400 million years old.

The Arachnid Family

The scorpion's closest relatives are spiders, mites, and ticks. Scientists estimate that there are more than 37,000 types of spiders. The smallest one is called *Patu marplesi*. Its entire body is about the size of the period that ends this sentence. The largest spider is the goliath birdeater tarantula. It grows to be about the size of a dinner plate.

Spiders are found in every type of **climate** and live everywhere from deserts to oceans. They come in almost every color imaginable and in many sizes and shapes.

Mites and ticks are very small, but they can cause big problems. Although they're more likely to bother plants, insects, and animals, mites can cause allergic reactions and severe itching in humans. Ticks are a bigger problem for people. They are responsible for spreading Lyme disease, which is a very serious illness.

Like scorpions, tarantulas look dangerous, but many people keep them as pets.

Very Scary Looking

Scorpions may look terrifying, but most aren't dangerous to humans. There are more than 1,500 scorpion species, but only around 25 of them can kill a person.

A healthy adult can usually survive a scorpion sting. However, young children, the elderly, and people who are already sick could suffer. Scorpion stings can lead to trouble breathing and swallowing, slurred speech, vision problems, and other symptoms. There are very few deaths in the United States from scorpion stings. However, death is more common in places without proper medical care. Serious scorpion stings are often treated with medicine that isn't available in developing countries or rural areas.

To avoid a scorpion sting, be careful when walking through areas where they like to live—and always wear shoes. Shake out clothing or shoes before putting them on. Scorpions like to hide in dark places!

FUN FACT! The Arizona bark scorpion is the most dangerous scorpion species found in the United States.

The Arizona bark scorpion lives in California, New Mexico, and Arizona.

CHAPTER 5

Nature's Helper

Scorpions play an important role in keeping ecosystems in balance. They help keep populations of pesky insects from getting too large. Scorpions are also an important source of food for other animals. Around the world, birds, lizards, and bats all rely on scorpions for food. Baboons, mongooses, and meerkats also make scorpions part of their diet.

Many of the scorpion's predators have learned that if they break off the scorpion's tail before trying to eat it, the scorpion will be harmless. Others are not bothered by scorpion venom.

Scientists have found that scorpions provide a good way to tell if an area is changing over time. Scorpions are very sensitive to the world around them. They also tend to live in one place for their whole life. This means that changes in the scorpion population might indicate there are also changes in the environment as a whole.

Birds are common predators of many scorpion species.

Medical Miracles

Scientists have discovered that scorpion venom can be used to help treat illnesses such as multiple sclerosis, diabetes, psoriasis, and arthritis. Scientists are conducting experiments to see if toxins from scorpion venom can be used to treat heart patients. Researchers believe scorpion venom might stop too much scar tissue from building up during the healing process after heart surgery.

Scorpion venom could even help fight cancer. In one study, researchers used a substance made from scorpion venom to make cancer cells glow. This glow shows doctors which tissue to remove. Other researchers used a toxin from the venom of a deathstalker scorpion to help with brain cancer treatment. Scorpion venom can even stop cancer cells from growing. Some of these treatments are still in the research stage. It is exciting to think that a feared creature could help save human lives.

Scorpions could one day provide solutions to important medical issues.

Words to Know

abdomen (AB-duh-muhn) — the rear section of an insect or arachnid's body

ancestor (AN-ses-tur) — ancient animal species that is related to modern species

arthropod (AHR-thruh-pahd) — an animal without a backbone that has a hard outer skeleton and three or more pairs of legs that can bend

carapace (KAHR-uh-pase) — a hard case or shield covering the back or part of the back of an animal

carnivores (KAHR-nuh-vorz) — animals that eat meat

cephalothorax (sef-uh-lo-THOR-aks) — the front section of an arachnid or higher crustacean

climate (KLYE-mit) — the weather typical of a place over long periods of time

dormant (DOR-muhnt) — inactive

ecosystems (EE-koh-sis-tuhmz) — communities that include all the living things in a place and their relation to the environment

exoskeleton (ek-so-SKEH-luh-tun) — an external supportive covering of an animal

fossils (FAH-suhlz) — bones, shells, or other traces of an animal or plant from millions of years ago, preserved as rock

litters (LIT-urz) — groups of baby animals that are born at the same time to the same mother

mate (MAYT) — to join together to produce babies

metabolism (muh-TAB-uh-liz-uhm) — the rate at which nutrients and energy are used to maintain body functions

molted (MOHL-tid) — shed old fur, feathers, or skin so that new ones can grow

organs (OR-guhnz) — parts of the body, such as the heart or the kidneys, that have a certain purpose

paleontologists (pay-lee-uhn-TAH-luh-jists) — scientists who study fossils and other ancient life-forms

paralyze (PAR-uh-lize) — to cause a loss of the power to move or feel a part of the body

predator (PREH-duh-tur) — an animal that lives by hunting other animals for food

prey (PRAY) — an animal that's hunted by another animal for food

species (SPEE-sheez) — one of the groups into which animals and plants of the same genus are divided; members of the same species can mate and have offspring

venom (VEH-num) — poison produced by some animals

Habitat Map

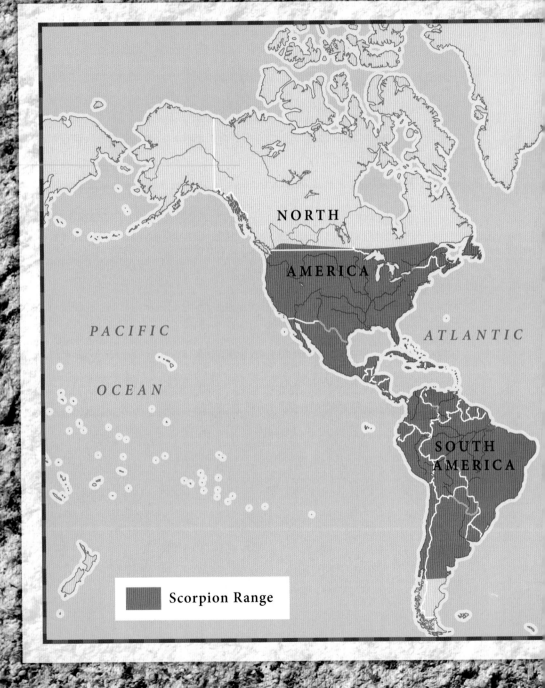

NORTH
AMERICA

PACIFIC

OCEAN

ATLANTIC

SOUTH
AMERICA

Scorpion Range

ARCTIC OCEAN

EUROPE

ASIA

AFRICA

PACIFIC OCEAN

CEAN

INDIAN

OCEAN

AUSTRALIA

Find Out More

Books

Eamer, Claire. *Spiked Scorpions & Walking Whales*. New York: Annick Press Ltd., 2009.

Gonzales, Doreen. *Scorpions in the Dark*. New York: PowerKids Press, 2010.

Markle, Sandra. *Scorpions: Armed Stingers*. Minneapolis: Lerner, 2011.

Pringle, Laurence. *Scorpions! Strange and Wonderful*. Honesdale, PA: Boyds Mills Press, 2013.

Visit this Scholastic Web site for more information on scorpions:
www.factsfornow.scholastic.com
Enter the keyword **Scorpions**

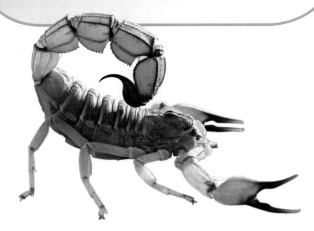

Index

Page numbers in *italics* indicate a photograph or map.

(Index continued)

About the Author

Vicky Franchino has never seen a scorpion in person, but she has seen a really neat Scholastic book called *The Real Thing! Scorpions*, which has an actual scorpion embedded in its cover! How cool is that? If Vicky lived in a place that had scorpions, she would be checking her shoes every day (read this book to find out why!). Vicky lives with her family in Madison, Wisconsin—a place where scorpions only live in cages.
Photo by Kat Franchino